RICHARD COEUR DE LION AND BLONDEL

RICHARD COEUR DE LION AND BLONDEL

CHARLOTTE BRONTË

A BRONTË BOOK

Published by Wildside Press LLC.
www.wildsidebooks.com

All that is written in this book, must be in a good, plain and legible hand. —P.B.

CONTENTS

RICHARD CŒUR DE LION
AND BLONDEL

The blush, the light, the gorgeous glow of Eve
Waned from the radiant chambers of the west;
Now, twilight's robe, dim, orient shadows weave:
One star, gleams faintly lustrous, in the east;
Far down it shines, on the blue Danube's breast,
As calmly, wavelessly its waters glide
On to th' appointed regions of their rest,
The Sea, profound and hoary, waste and wide;
Whose black'ning billows swell in ever restless pride.

High o'er the river rose a rocky hill,
With barren sides, precipitous, and steep:
There, 'gainst the sunset heav'ns, serene, and still
Frown'd the dark turrets of a feudal Keep.
Its folded flag, hung in the air asleep;
The breathless beauty of the Summer night
Gave not that Austrian [folio 2] standard, to the sweep
Of fresh'ning Zepyr, or wild Storm-blast's might;
But motionless, it drooped, in eve's soft, dying light

In that Stern Fortess, there were arch, and tow'r,
And Iron-wrought lattice, narrow, deep-embaye'd;
Where the gloom gather'd thick as night's mid hour
And round about it, hung a chilling shade,
Which told of dungeons, where the light ne'er play'd,
Of prison-walls, of fetter-bolt and chain;

Of Captives, 'neath a Tyrant's durance laid;
Never, to view the sun's bright face again;
Never to breathe the air, of free, wild hill and plain.

The moon had risen, a host of stars among,
When, to th' embattled castle walls, drew nigh
A wand'ring minstrel, from his shoulders hung
A harp, sweet instrument of melody.
He paus'd awhile, beneath the turret high,
Then took his harp, and all [folio 3] the sweet chords
swept,
Till a sound swell'd beneath the silent sky,
And holiest music, on the charmed air crept,
Waked from the magic strings, Where till that hour they
slept.

O! how that wild strain o'er the river swelled,
And mingled with its gentle murmuring,
From the true fount of Song divine, it welled;
Music's own simple undefiled spring;
Notes rose, and dyed such as the wild birds sing
In the lone-wood, or the far lonelier sky.
O! none but Blondel but the minstrel king
Could waken such transcendant melody;
Sweet as a fairy's lute, soft as a passing sigh.

The strain he sung, was some antique romance,
Some long forgotten song of other years;
Born in the cloudless clime of sunny France,
Where Earth, in vernal loveliness appears;
Where the bright grape [folio 4] distils its purple tears;
And clear streams flow, and dim, blue hills arise
A gleaming crown of snows Each mountain wears;

And there are cities, 'neath her starry skies,
As fair as ever blest, with beauty, mortal eyes.

BLONDEL'S SONG.

The moonlight; sleeps low, on the hills of Provence;
The stars are all tracking, their paths in the sky:
How softly, and brightly, their golden orbs glance,
Where the long shining waves, of the silver Rhone lie

The tow'rs of De Courcy rise high in the beam,
From sky to earth trembling, so lustrous and pale,
Around them there dwells the deep hush of a dream,
And stilled is the murmur of River, and Gale.

There are groves in the moonlight, all sparkling with dew,
There are dim garden-paths, round that Castle of Pride;
Where the bud of the rose, and the hyacinth blue, [folio 5]
Close their leaves, to the balm, of the moist even-tide.
And long is the alley, dark, bowery, and dim,
Where sits a white form 'neath a tall chestnut tree
Which waves its brown branches, all dark'ling and grim,
O'er the young Rose of Courcy, Sweet Anna Marie.

And who kneels beside her? A warrior in mail.
On his helm there's a plume In his hand there's a lance
And why does the cheek of the lady turn pale?
Why weeps in her beauty The Flower of Provence?

She weeps for her lover, this night, are they met
To breathe a farewell, 'Neath love's own holy star;
For to-morrow the crest of the young Lavalette,

Will float highest, and first in the van of the war.

Thus far sung Blondel, when a sudden tone,
of quivering harp-strings, on his ear upsprung;
It sounded, like an echo of his own:
So faintly, that mysterious [folio 6] music rung,
So sweet, it floated, those dark towers among,
And seemed to issue from their topmost height;
Then there were words, in measured cadence sung.
Now soft and low, then with a master's might,
Poured forth that varying strain, upon the stilly night

Who sings? the minstrel knows there is but one,
Whose voice has music half so rich, and deep
Whose hand can summon from the harp a tone,
So thrilling, that it calls from latent sleep
Heroic thoughts, dims eyes, that seldom weep,
With tears of extasy, and fires the breast,
Till listening warriors, from their chargers leap,
Assume the glittering helm, and nodding crest,
Unsheathe the ready sword And lay the lance in rest

But not of war, nor of the battle blast,
Sung now the kingly harper. No his strain
Was mournful, as a dream [folio 7] of days long past.
At times it swelled, but quickly died again;
And oh! the sadness of that wild refrain!
Suited full well with the lone, solemn hour,
Too sad for joy, too exquisite for pain,
It touched the heart Subdued the spirit's power
Blent with the Danube's moan, and wailed around the
tower

RICHARD'S SONG

Thrice, the great fadeless lights of heaven
The moon, and the eternal sun
As God's unchanging law was given,
Have each their course appointed run.
Three times the Earth, her mighty way
Hath measured o'er a shoreless sea;
While hopeless still from day, to day,
I've sat in lone captivity;
Listening the wind, and River's moan,
Wakening my wild harp's solemn tone,
   And longing to be free.

Blondel! my heart seems [folio 8] cold, and dead;
My soul, has lost its ancient might;
The sun of chivalry is fled
And dark despair's, unholy night
Above me closes still and deep;
While wearily each lapsing day
Leads onward, to the last, long sleep;
The hour when all shall pass away;
When King, and Captive, Lord, and Slave
Must rest unparted, in the grave
   A mass of soulless clay.

O long I've listened to the sound,
Of winter's blast, and summer's breeze,
As their sweet voices sung around,

Through echoing caves, and wind-waved trees.
And long I've viewed from prison bars
Sunset, and dawn, and night, and noon:
Watched the uprising of the stars,
Seen the calm advent of the moon:
But blast and breeze and star, and Sun
All vainly swept, [folio 9] all vainly shone,
        I filled a living tomb.

God of my fathers! Can it be?
Must I, the chosen of thy might?
Whose name alone, brought victory,
Whose battle cry was God my Right
Closed, in a Tyrant's dungeon cell,
Wear out the remnant of my life?
And never hear again, the swell
Of high and hot and glorious strife
Where trumpet's peal, and bugles sing,
And minstrels sweep the martial string,
        And war, and fame are rife.

No Blondel! thou wert sent by heaven,
Thy King, thy Lion-King to free,
To thee, the high command was given
To rescue from captivity.
Haste from the Tyrant Austrian's Hold,
Cross rapidly the rolling sea, [folio 10]
And go, where dwell the brave, the bold,
By stream and Hill and green-wood tree.
Minstrel let merry England, ring
With tidings of her Lion-King,
        And bring back liberty.

Such was the lay, the monarch-minstrel sung,
A few bright moons, waned from the silent heavens
And Albion, with a shout of Triumph rung;
As once again her worshipped King, was given
Back to her breast, his bonds asunder riven
And the Sweet Empress of the subject Sea
Sent up her hymn of gratitude to heaven
Through all her coasts she hailed him crowned and free
The Champion of God's hosts The pride of liberty.

Charlotte Brontë
Dec^{br} 27th 1833
Haworth n^r Bradford

ABOUT THE AUTHOR

Charlotte Brontë (1816 – 1855) was an English novelist and poet, the eldest of the three Brontë sisters who survived into adulthood and whose novels have become classics of English literature. She first published her works (including her best known novel, Jane Eyre) under the pen name Currer Bell.

www.ingramcontent.com/pod-product-compliance
Lightning Source LLC
Chambersburg PA
CBHW021124020426
42331CB00004B/620